MADE WITH LOVE
BY

I love when you

_____

_____

_____

_____

You taught me how to

_____

_____

_____

_____

It's amazing how you

_____

_____

_____

_____

I love your

_____

_____

_____

_____

You are good at

_____

_____

_____

_____

## Funniest thing you do is

_____

_____

_____

_____

You are a perfect

You always have
time to

_____

_____

_____

_____

I love you
because

_____

_____

_____

_____

## You give me the best

_____

_____

_____

_____

You work hard at

I'm impressed by your

_____

_____

_____

_____

## You motivate me to

Iam so happy you made me

_____

_____

_____

_____

## It makes me smile when

_____

_____

_____

_____

# I'm proud to say you are

_____

_____

_____

_____

You deserve the

You are happiest when

_____

_____

_____

_____

I love how you never

_____

_____

_____

_____

I love you because

_____

_____

_____

_____

You were right
about

_____

_____

_____

_____

I love you more
than

_____

_____

_____

_____

I love how you
always

_____

_____

_____

_____

## You made me feel special when

_____

_____

_____

_____

I will always be grateful for your

_____

_____

_____

_____

## A time we've laughed the hardest was

_____

_____

_____

_____

You could win a talent show with your

_____

_____

_____

_____

I want you to
know that you
are

_____

_____

_____

_____

I love the pleasure you take in

_____

_____

_____

_____

I love when you
tell stories about

_____

_____

_____

_____

We always have
the best time
when we

_____

_____

_____

_____

## Best thing about your job is

_____

_____

_____

_____

I love getting your
advice on

_____

_____

_____

_____

Thanks for
encouraging me to

_____

_____

_____

_____

I love your
attitude towards

_____

_____

_____

_____

I admire your dedication to

_____

_____

_____

_____

## Four words that describe you

_____

_____

_____

_____

I love how you
always say

_____

_____

_____

_____

## This is what we have in common

_____

_____

_____

_____

## Your funniest joke was

You gave me the courage to

_____

_____

_____

_____

## You are special to me because

I never get tired of your

_____

_____

_____

_____

My favorite thing
about you is

_____

_____

_____

_____

I value your
advice about

_____

_____

_____

_____

## Our favorite thing to do is

_____

_____

_____

_____

You will always be my

I wish we have
more time to

_____

_____

_____

_____

I love how you

_____

_____

_____

_____

## I can't forget when

_____

_____

_____

_____

I smile when you

_____

_____

_____

_____

I love it when you

_____

_____

_____

_____

## I like when you call me

_____

_____

_____

_____

## You make me laugh when

_____

_____

_____

_____

I wish i have your

Thankyou for

_____

_____

_____

_____

You always help me to

_____

_____

_____

_____

We have so much
fun when

_____

_____

_____

_____

You inspire me to

_____

_____

_____

_____

You like to

_____

_____

_____

_____

Made in the USA
Monee, IL
02 December 2021

83704470R00035